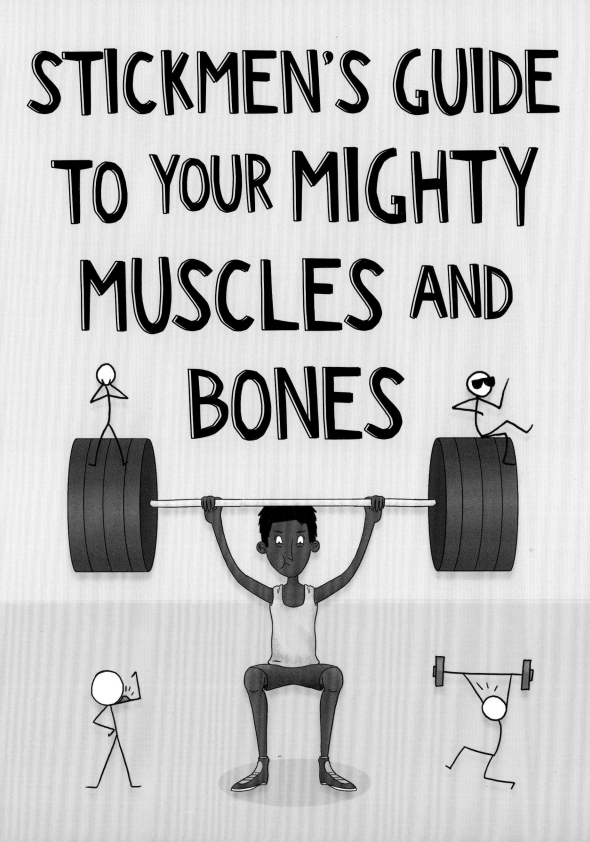

Thanks to the creative team:
Senior Editor: Alice Peebles
Fact Checking: Kate Mitchell
Design: www.collaborate.agency

Hungry Tomato®
A division of Lerner Publishing Group, Inc.
241 First Avenue North
Minneapolis, MN 55401 USA

For reading levels and more information, look up this title at www.lernerbooks.com.

Main body text set in Avenir Next Medium 9.5/12.
Typeface provided by Linotype AG

Library of Congress Cataloging-in-Publication Data

Names: Farndon, John, author. | Dean, Venitia, 1976- illustrator.
Title: Stickmen's guide to your mighty muscles and bones / John Farndon ; illustrated by Venitia Dean.
Other titles: Your mighty muscles and bones
Description: Minneapolis : Hungry Tomato, [2017] | Series: Stickmen's guides to your awesome body | Audience: Ages 8-12. | Audience: Grades 4 to 6. | Includes index.
Identifiers: LCCN 2016046939 (print) | LCCN 2016050330 (ebook) | ISBN 9781512432145 (lb : alk. paper) | ISBN 9781512450118 (eb pdf)
Subjects: LCSH: Musculoskeletal system—Juvenile literature. | Muscles—Juvenile literature. | Bones—Juvenile literature.
Classification: LCC QP321 .F37 2017 (print) | LCC QP321 (ebook) | DDC 612.7—dc23

LC record available at https://lccn.loc.gov/2016046939

Manufactured in the United States of America
1-41769-23530-1/9/2017

STICKMEN'S GUIDE TO YOUR MIGHTY MUSCLES AND BONES

by John Farndon
Illustrated by Venitia Dean

HUNGRY TOMATO®

Minneapolis

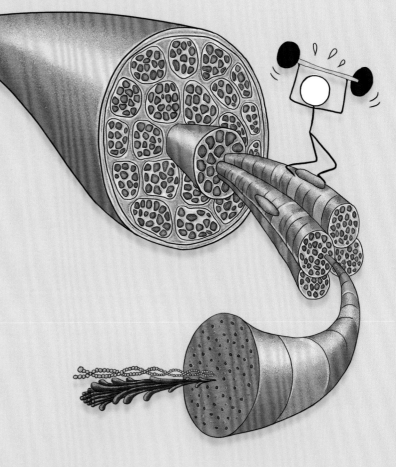

There are more than
23,000 fibers in just
one of the muscles in
your arm!

Contents

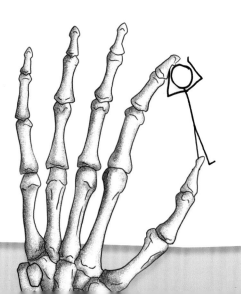

Introduction

Although your body seems very complicated, it all begins to make sense if you think of it in terms of systems, each with its own task to do. Some systems, such as the nervous system (the body's communication system), extend throughout the body. It is the task of the skeleton, the body's framework of bones, to protect you and keep you upright. The skeleton also works with muscles, which give your body the ability to move.

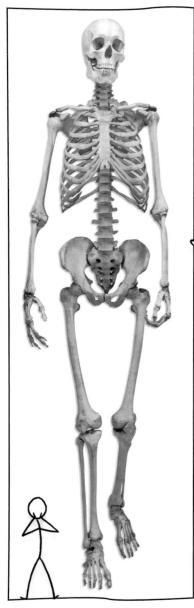

Skeleton

The skeleton is the part of the body that may last the longest after a person dies. That's because the bones are made from tough minerals that don't quickly rot away. Altogether, over 100 billion people have lived on Earth so far. That means there could be 100 billion skeletons lying around. Fortunately, most do crumble into dust eventually!

Lucy

The world's most famous skeleton is about 3.2 million years old! It's called Lucy and is the skeleton of a small ancestor of humans called an australopithecine. It was found in Ethiopia in 1974. Its shape shows that even this long ago, our ancestors walked upright on two feet.

Muscles

You have over 600 muscles on the outside of your skeleton. If they could all pull together, they could lift a bus! Of course, that could never happen because they all pull in different directions. The average adult man can just about lift another adult off the ground.

The Strongest Man

The world's strongest man ever was Canadian Louis Cyr, who lived between 1863 and 1912. He could push a railroad truck uphill, beat two horses in a tug of war, and lift the weight of five adults with his little finger. His most famous feat was the backlift, in which he lifted a bench with eighteen men on it on his back.

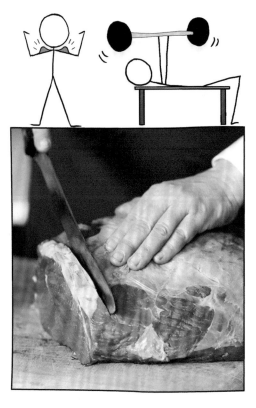

Meaty Muscle

If you want to know what your muscles look like on the inside, go to the butcher. When you eat meat, you're eating mostly the muscle of animals. Only fat, gristle, and bone are not muscle. If you ever eat steak, chances are you'll be eating the big rump, or bottom muscles, of a cow. Your own bottom muscles look similar!

Holding You Together

If you looked through a powerful microscope, you would see that your body is made of tiny living packets called cells—about 37 trillion altogether! And just as lots of bricks make a wall, so lots of cells joined together make different kinds of tissue. Tissues are the basic building materials of your body.

Four Tissues

There are four kinds of tissue. Most of you is either muscle tissue—the tissue that makes muscle—or connective tissue, which fills the spaces between muscles and other tissues. But there is also epithelial tissue that lines and wraps things, and nervous tissue that makes up the nervous system, your body's Internet.

nervous tissue makes up your nerves and brain

epithelial tissue lines your airways and blood vessels and wraps your heart

connective tissue comes in various kinds, including bone, tendon, cartilage, fat, and blood

Connective Tissue

Connective tissue is made of three things: cells, thin fibers, and a matrix. The matrix is basically just a setting for the other materials, like the bread in a currant loaf. It can be anything from a runny syrup to a thick gel.

muscle tissue is the special fibers that make things move

Smooth Muscle

There are different kinds of muscle. Smooth muscles are the ones deep inside your body. They form tubes or bags and move things around by squeezing. For example, rings of smooth muscle squeeze food through your gut.

Skeletal Muscle

Skeletal muscles are all the muscles you see under your skin, covering your skeleton. They are sometimes called striated muscles. *Striated* means "stripy," and these muscles get their name because under a microscope, you can see dark bands around them.

Cardiac Muscle

Cardiac muscle makes the strong walls of your heart. It squeezes automatically one hundred or so times a minute to pump blood around your body.

Do it Yourself

When you decide to jump and kick, your skeletal muscles make it happen. YOU can move these muscles if you want to, so they are called voluntary muscles. But you have little control over the heart and other muscles inside your body, so they are called involuntary muscles.

Your Muscly Body

Your body is covered with skeletal muscles. These are all bundles of fibers that tense and relax to move parts of your body. They range from big muscles, such as those in your bottom and legs, to tiny muscles, such as those in your ears.

The Skeletal Muscles

You have 640 skeletal muscles altogether, and they make up two-fifths of your weight. In these diagrams, you only see the muscles on the surface, but there are several layers underneath too. Some are long with a bulge in the middle, some are triangular, and some are sheetlike.

a major neck muscle, the sternocleidomastoid, tilts your head to either side

the pectoral turns your arm

the biceps raises your arm

the triceps lowers your arm

the external oblique holds your side in

the sartorius moves both the hip and knee joint

the sartorius is the longest muscle in the body

the quadriceps bends your knee

Long Muscle

The sartorius runs over the hip and down over the knee and turns the thigh. It gets its name from the Latin word *sartor*, meaning "tailor." That's because tailors used to stretch this muscle when sitting cross-legged to work.

the shin muscle lowers your foot

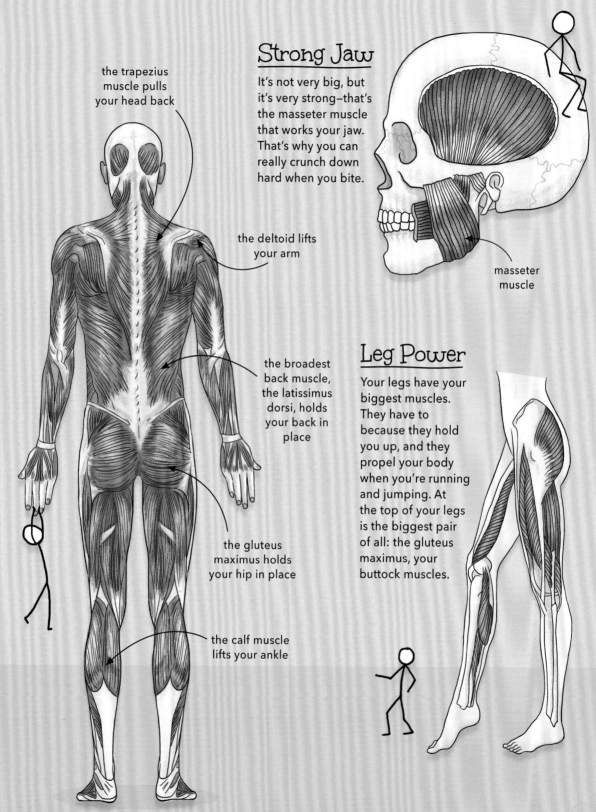

the trapezius muscle pulls your head back

Strong Jaw

It's not very big, but it's very strong—that's the masseter muscle that works your jaw. That's why you can really crunch down hard when you bite.

the deltoid lifts your arm

masseter muscle

the broadest back muscle, the latissimus dorsi, holds your back in place

Leg Power

Your legs have your biggest muscles. They have to because they hold you up, and they propel your body when you're running and jumping. At the top of your legs is the biggest pair of all: the gluteus maximus, your buttock muscles.

the gluteus maximus holds your hip in place

the calf muscle lifts your ankle

11

Pulling Together

Your muscles make your body move in all kinds of ways. But they do it all just by pulling themselves shorter (contracting) or relaxing. Each muscle works simply by pulling two bones together, so they must be anchored to bones at both ends.

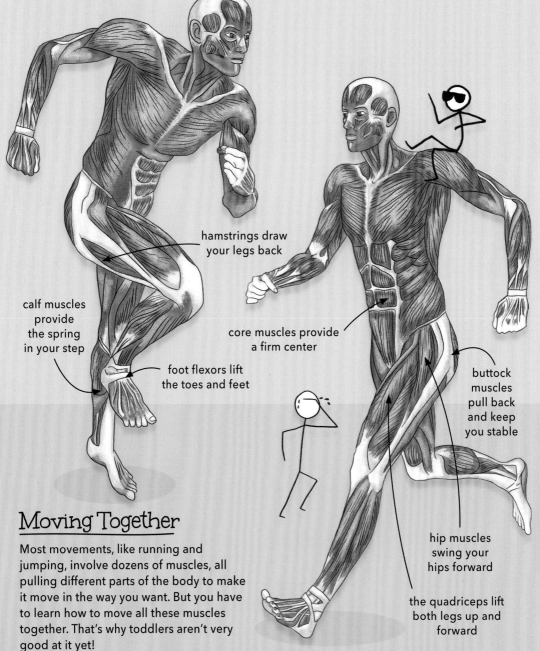

hamstrings draw your legs back

calf muscles provide the spring in your step

core muscles provide a firm center

foot flexors lift the toes and feet

buttock muscles pull back and keep you stable

hip muscles swing your hips forward

the quadriceps lift both legs up and forward

Moving Together

Most movements, like running and jumping, involve dozens of muscles, all pulling different parts of the body to make it move in the way you want. But you have to learn how to move all these muscles together. That's why toddlers aren't very good at it yet!

Muscle Pairs

Muscles can make themselves shorter, but they cannot make themselves longer. So each time a muscle pulls shorter, it must be pulled back by another muscle shortening in the opposite direction. That's why muscles are arranged in pairs, with a flexor to bend a joint and an extensor to straighten it out.

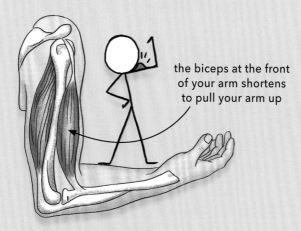

the biceps at the front of your arm shortens to pull your arm up

the triceps at the back of your arm shortens to pull your arm down again

Push-ups

Push-ups are one of the simplest and most effective forms of exercise, which is why they are very popular with people who want to stay fit. They involve most of the muscles in the upper body, including those in the arms, chest, and abdomen.

deltoids are the shoulder muscles that provide a firm base for the arms

pectorals are the large upper chest muscles that really take the strain

abdominal muscles help to hold the body steady

13

Inside a Muscle

Skeletal muscles get their strength from bundles of fibers that stretch from one end of the muscle to the other. Some muscles are made from just a few hundred fibers. Others are made from hundreds of thousands. But their superpower is getting shorter!

bundle of muscle fibers

muscle fiber

myofibril

Muscle Fibers

Muscles are made up of fibers, which are actually long cells. Each fiber is made from many even thinner threads called myofibrils. These are made from thin threads of two proteins: actin and myosin.

actin

myosin

Power Packs

Myofibrils are made up of tiny power packs called sarcomeres. Inside them, thin, twisty strands of actin interlock with thicker, smoother strands of myosin. When you want to move, a nerve signal tells the muscle to act. At once, hooks on the myosin twist sharply and pull on the actin, shortening the muscle.

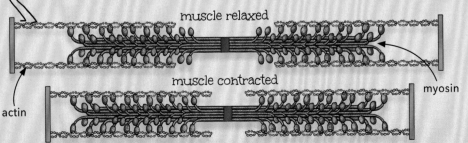

muscle relaxed

muscle contracted

actin

myosin

Pulling or Holding

When a muscle moves part of the body, it shortens. This happens when you run, for example, and is called an isotonic contraction. Sometimes the muscles can pull to hold the body in place without getting shorter. This is an isometric contraction.

Pulling
(isotonic contraction)

Holding
(isometric contraction)

tendon

muscle contracts and shortens

muscle contracts but does not shorten

Holding Weight

When muscles contract, they can shorten by almost half their length. When muscles work isometrically, however, they simply get fatter and stay the same length. This happens when weight lifters hold the bar up above their bodies.

How to Get Strong

Top athletes train hard to get strong. They work hard at exercises that make their muscles grow and become better able to keep pulling. If muscles aren't used, they gradually become weaker.

Weight Training

When you exercise, you get fitter and stronger. Regular exercise improves fitness by bulking up your muscles, strengthening your heart, and building up your body's ability to pump blood and supply muscles with oxygen. Weight lifters concentrate on building up their muscles for maximum strength. Marathon runners focus on endurance.

How a weight lifter's body shape changes as the muscles grow

Muscle Growth

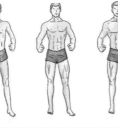

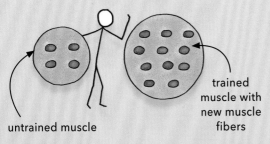

trained muscle with new muscle fibers

untrained muscle

When you exercise, your muscles grow larger. At first, the fibers just grow fatter. But if you go on exercising regularly, you grow new fibers, so your muscles grow stronger. The blood supply to the muscles improves too, so they can work for longer.

Fast or Slow?

Muscle fibers come in two kinds: white and red. Each kind pulls, or twitches, at different rates. Sprinters have lots of white fibers that twitch rapidly to give a burst of action. Marathon runners develop slow-twitch red fibers that keep working longer.

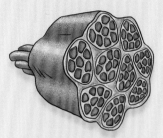 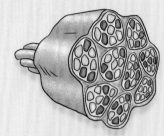 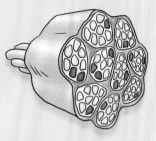

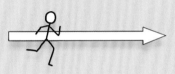 slow reds for marathons

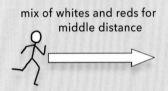 mix of whites and reds for middle distance

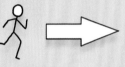 fast whites for sprints

Air Power

Muscle cells get their power from sugar in your food and from the oxygen you breathe. On a long bike ride, they work slowly and aerobically. That means muscles work gently enough to take in air as they go. But when you sprint, your muscles work so fast your body can't deliver enough fresh oxygen. So they briefly work anaerobically (without air).

Cramps

If you're out of shape, your muscles go on working anaerobically longer. Lactic acid builds up, making your muscles feel sore. You might also get cramps. A cramp is a painful twinge in your muscles. It is set off when the nerves that trigger them fire randomly. This is usually because of a temporary shortage of the minerals your nerves need to work properly.

Your Framework of Bones

Under your skin and muscles, you have a strong framework of bones called a skeleton. It holds your body together; provides anchor points for the muscles you use to move; supports your skin and other tissues; and protects your heart, brain, and other organs.

cheekbone

collarbone

Human Skeleton

Your skeleton is made of over 200 bones. Your skull, spine, and ribcage make the axial skeleton. Your shoulders, arms, hands, hips, and legs are attached to this and are called the appendicular skeleton.

finger bones or phalanges

metacarpals

breastbone or sternum

Hand Bones

The hands each have twenty-seven bones, making up almost a quarter of all your bones. That's why hands can move in more ways than any other part of your body. The hand bones form joints at the knuckles.

wrist bones or carpals

thigh bone or femur

kneecap or patella

shin bone or tibia

Head Office

Humans have rounded skulls like no other animals. Experts can track how humans developed in the distant past from the changing shape of ancient skulls they have found. They can see how the top, or cranium, grew to allow room for a bigger brain.

calf bone or fibula

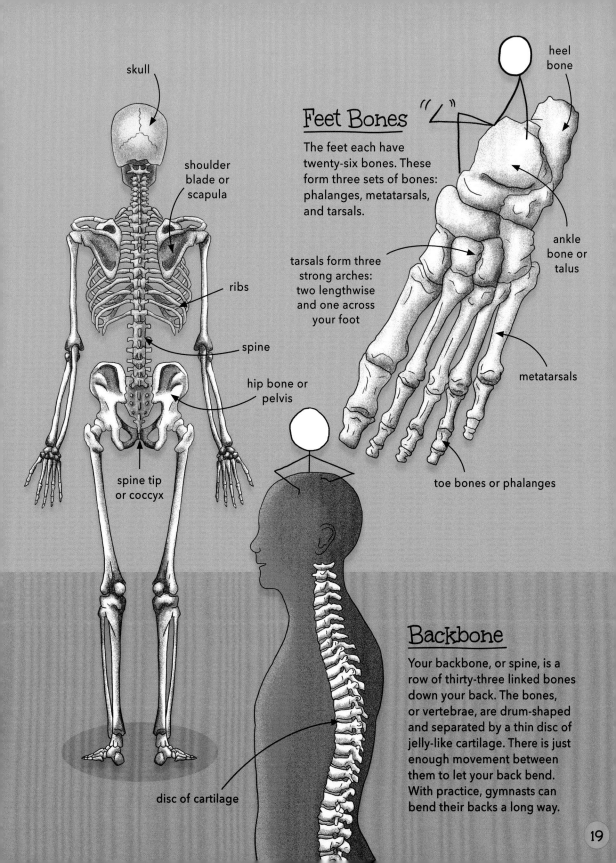

skull

shoulder blade or scapula

ribs

spine

hip bone or pelvis

spine tip or coccyx

disc of cartilage

heel bone

Feet Bones

The feet each have twenty-six bones. These form three sets of bones: phalanges, metatarsals, and tarsals.

tarsals form three strong arches: two lengthwise and one across your foot

ankle bone or talus

metatarsals

toe bones or phalanges

Backbone

Your backbone, or spine, is a row of thirty-three linked bones down your back. The bones, or vertebrae, are drum-shaped and separated by a thin disc of jelly-like cartilage. There is just enough movement between them to let your back bend. With practice, gymnasts can bend their backs a long way.

Strong Bones

Bones are really light because they're partly hollow. But they're superstrong too because they're made of both hard minerals and stretchy fibers that keep them from snapping.

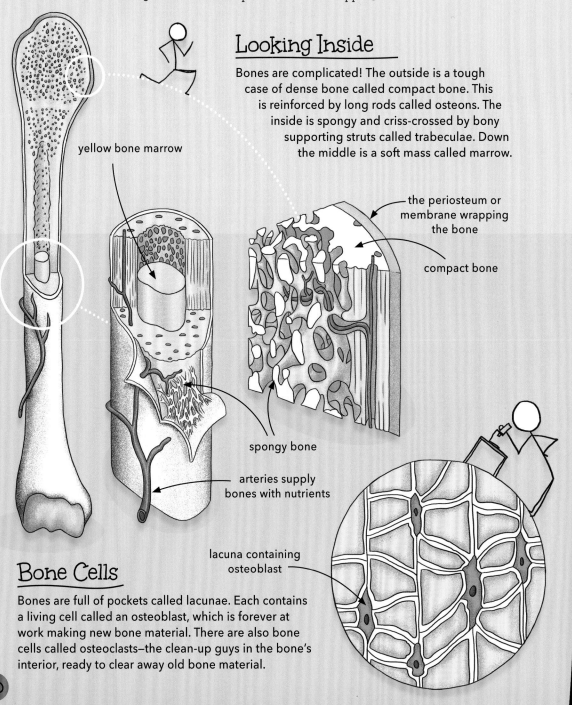

yellow bone marrow

Looking Inside

Bones are complicated! The outside is a tough case of dense bone called compact bone. This is reinforced by long rods called osteons. The inside is spongy and criss-crossed by bony supporting struts called trabeculae. Down the middle is a soft mass called marrow.

the periosteum or membrane wrapping the bone

compact bone

spongy bone

arteries supply bones with nutrients

lacuna containing osteoblast

Bone Cells

Bones are full of pockets called lacunae. Each contains a living cell called an osteoblast, which is forever at work making new bone material. There are also bone cells called osteoclasts—the clean-up guys in the bone's interior, ready to clear away old bone material.

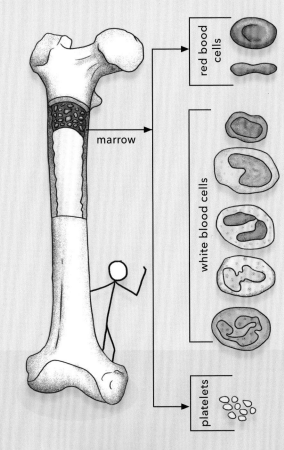

marker: marrow

red blood cells

white blood cells

platelets

Blood Factory

The hollow center of your bones contains a soft, spongy substance called marrow. Some is red and bloody, and some is yellow and fatty. Red marrow is the body's blood factory, churning out new blood cells nonstop.

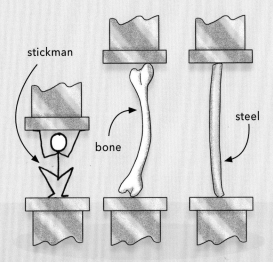

stickman

bone

steel

Bone vs. Steel

People sometimes say that bone is stronger than steel, weight for weight! That's not quite true: steel is stronger and bone is also very light, so a rod of steel the same size would be much stronger than bone. All the same, bone is both strong and very light—just what you need for moving around.

Broken Bones

Bones are strong, but sometimes they do get broken. Amazingly, broken bones can heal. First the body stops any bleeding. Then proteins bring in osteoclasts to clear away the debris, so the osteoblasts can begin to create new bone material to heal the break.

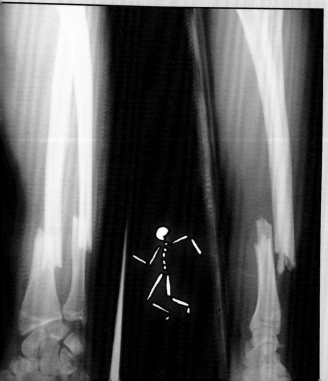

Moving Parts

Even though it is incredibly strong, your skeleton can bend and move in almost any direction, thanks to its joints. Joints are where bones meet. All your bones, except one in the throat, form a joint with another bone.

Swivel Joint

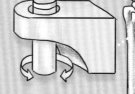

The swivel joint in your neck allows you to turn your head to the left and right.

Hinge Joints

The hinge joints in your fingers, elbows, ankles, and toes swing in only two directions, just like a door on hinges—but they are very strong. You use hinge joints when you make a fist or curl your toes.

Ellipsoidal Joints

There is an ellipsoidal joint at the base of each index finger. It lets you bend and extend this finger, and rock it from side to side.

Ball-and-Socket Joints

Your hip and shoulder joints are your most flexible joints. They are ball-and-socket joints, which let you swing your arms and legs in lots of different directions.

Saddle Joints

The joint at the base of each thumb is a saddle joint. In these, two saddle-shaped bones fit snugly together and can rock back and forth and from side to side. They are strong, but they can't rotate much.

Gliding Joints

Where two flat bones are held together by ligaments just loosely enough to glide past each other, it's called a gliding joint. Some of the bones in your wrists and ankles move like this.

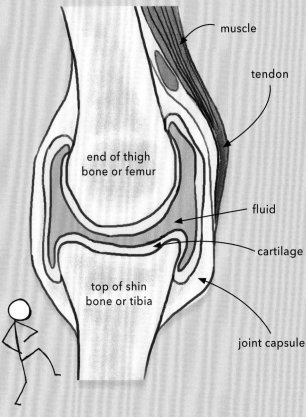

muscle

tendon

end of thigh bone or femur

fluid

cartilage

top of shin bone or tibia

joint capsule

Knee Joint

Your knee is a special hinge joint. It can bend like all hinge joints, but it can also rotate slightly. It is protected by a little shield of bone called the kneecap and surrounded by a capsule of rubbery cartilage and fluid to cushion and lubricate it.

Knee Injury

Knee joints are particularly vulnerable to damage. Many athletes suffer knee injuries that bring about major career setbacks. One of the most common is ligament injury caused by turning the knee sharply.

Bending Bones?

Ligaments usually limit the movement of your skeleton. But with practice, some contortionists are able to bend their bodies into all kinds of strange shapes. But the bones are not bending—it is just the joints moving farther than normal.

Binders

Bones are tied together and muscles are tied to bones with short, strong fibers called ligaments and tendons. Ligaments are attached to the bones on either side of a joint to bind them together. Tendons anchor muscles to bones.

Hand Holding

Your hand contains lots of strong ligaments and tendons to give you a strong grip. The muscles that move your fingers are not in your hand at all—they're in your arm and are connected by tendons. If you spread your fingers out, you can see these tendons clearly as ridges in the back of your hand.

pretendinous bands pull your fingers up

abductor muscles in the palm spread your hands

the palmaris longus tendon runs from a muscle in your arm to your hand

shoulder blade

triceps

Arm Bands

The muscles in your arm are attached to bones via tendons at either end. The biceps is attached with a tendon to a part of the radius bone called the radial tuberosity, a small bump on the bone near your elbow joint.

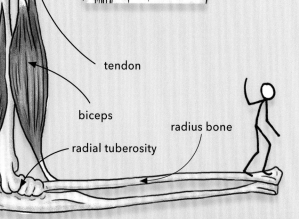

tendon

biceps

radius bone

radial tuberosity

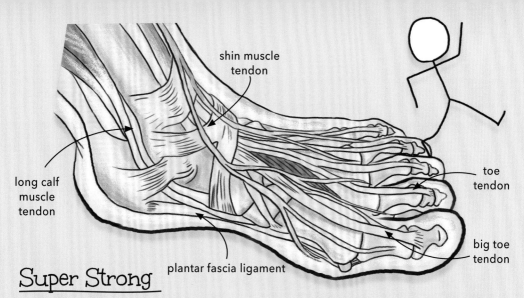

shin muscle
tendon

toe
tendon

long calf
muscle
tendon

big toe
tendon

plantar fascia ligament

Super Strong

The tendons and ligaments in your feet have to be especially strong since they must bear
your entire weight and provide the spring in your foot for running and jumping. The key
ligament is the plantar fascia, which gives your foot its arch. By stretching and contracting, it
allows the arch to curve or flatten so you can balance and walk.

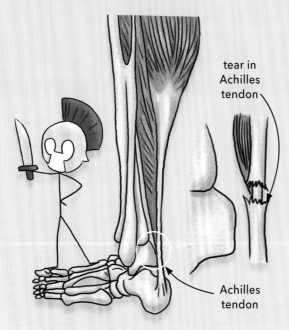

tear in
Achilles
tendon

Achilles
tendon

Achilles Heel

When the ancient Greek hero Achilles was
a baby, his mother dipped him in a magic
river to make him immortal. But the water
never reached the place on his heel where
she held him. Later, he died in battle from a
wound inflicted there. That's why the tendon
holding your foot is called the Achilles
tendon–but it is actually pretty strong!

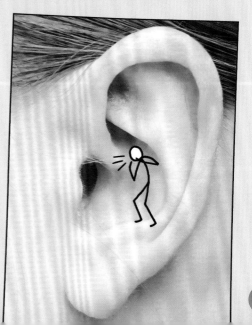

Cartilaginous Joints

Cartilage is a rubbery material that cushions
the ends of bones and keeps them from being
damaged. And under your skin, your ears
and nose are made of a special kind of extra
bendy cartilage called elastic cartilage.

Bonehead

Your skull is the tough dome of bone that protects your brain. It looks like a single bone, but it is actually made from twenty-two bones held together by rigid joints called sutures.

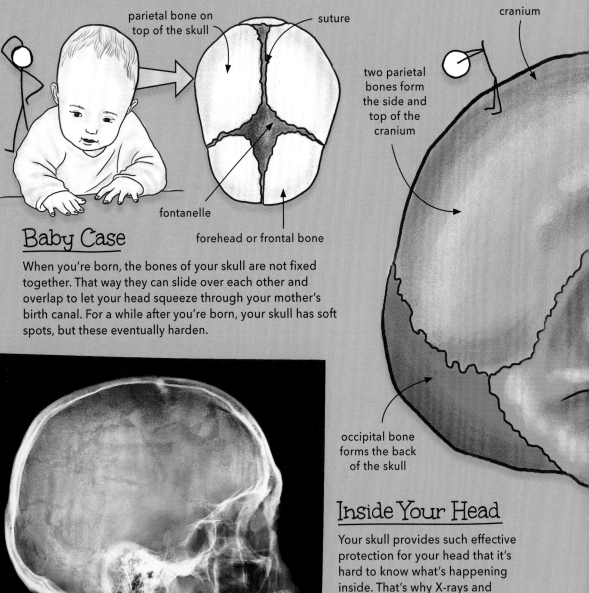

parietal bone on top of the skull

suture

cranium

two parietal bones form the side and top of the cranium

fontanelle

forehead or frontal bone

Baby Case

When you're born, the bones of your skull are not fixed together. That way they can slide over each other and overlap to let your head squeeze through your mother's birth canal. For a while after you're born, your skull has soft spots, but these eventually harden.

occipital bone forms the back of the skull

Inside Your Head

Your skull provides such effective protection for your head that it's hard to know what's happening inside. That's why X-rays and brain scans are so important. They allow doctors and scientists to see inside, check for damage, and learn more about what's going on.

Nut Case

The dome at the top of your head that holds your brain is called the cranium. It's made of eight curved pieces of bone fused together along sutures. The rest of the skull contains the fourteen bones of your face. This includes your lower jaw, the only bone in your skull that moves.

Hole in the Head

In ancient times, many people were trepanned. This meant drilling a large hole in the skull. It was very dangerous and must have been incredibly painful. No one knows just why they did it. Maybe they thought it would stop seizures or let evil spirits out.

two temporal bones on the side of the skull house the ear structures

suture

forehead or frontal bone protects the brain and supports the face

eye socket

nose bone

cheekbone

Helmet

Your skull provides very strong protection for your brain. Yet even your skull may not be enough if you hit your head hard. That's why safety helmets are important when you ride a bike or play sports where you can fall or be hit.

upper jaw or maxilla

lower jaw or mandible

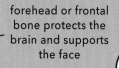

The History of Muscle and Bone

For a long time, scientists knew very little about muscle and bone. It seemed so obvious and simple that no one bothered to find out much. Only artists looked at muscles carefully, so they could understand how to draw people accurately. But gradually, scientists realized that there is quite a lot to learn about your skeleton and your muscles!

162 CE
The Roman physician Galen correctly identified the femur (thigh bone) as the longest and strongest bone in the body.

1630
The French thinker René Descartes began to look further into how muscles worked. He thought in terms of machines. He described muscles and tendons as "devices and springs which serve to set [nerves] in motion."

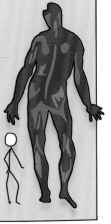

500 CE	1600	1700

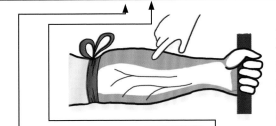

1653
The English doctor William Harvey was the first to describe muscles as bundles of fibers. He also understood that they gave their power by contracting and relaxing.

1510
The great Italian artist Leonardo da Vinci created amazingly accurate drawings of muscle and bone. He studied bodies with his extraordinary eye for detail. Electronic body scans have shown just how accurate da Vinci's drawings were.

1543
The Italian physician Andreas Vesalius was one of the first to cut up dead bodies in order to map them scientifically. His famous book, *On the Fabric of the Human Body*, contained the first detailed and accurate drawings of all the bones of the skeleton and all the muscles.

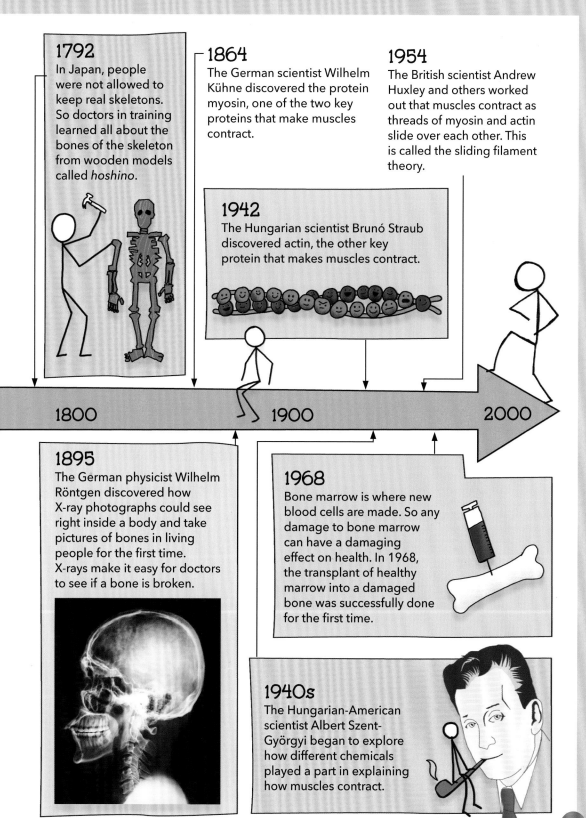

1792
In Japan, people were not allowed to keep real skeletons. So doctors in training learned all about the bones of the skeleton from wooden models called *hoshino*.

1864
The German scientist Wilhelm Kühne discovered the protein myosin, one of the two key proteins that make muscles contract.

1954
The British scientist Andrew Huxley and others worked out that muscles contract as threads of myosin and actin slide over each other. This is called the sliding filament theory.

1942
The Hungarian scientist Brunó Straub discovered actin, the other key protein that makes muscles contract.

1800

1900

2000

1895
The German physicist Wilhelm Röntgen discovered how X-ray photographs could see right inside a body and take pictures of bones in living people for the first time. X-rays make it easy for doctors to see if a bone is broken.

1968
Bone marrow is where new blood cells are made. So any damage to bone marrow can have a damaging effect on health. In 1968, the transplant of healthy marrow into a damaged bone was successfully done for the first time.

1940s
The Hungarian-American scientist Albert Szent-Györgyi began to explore how different chemicals played a part in explaining how muscles contract.

29

More Muscly and Bony Facts

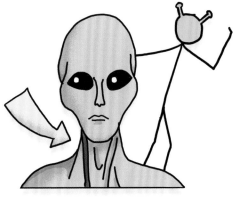

Neck and Neck

The sternocleidomastoid is a large muscle running down the side of your neck. It's pronounced stern-o-cly-doe-mass-toid. This is the muscle that swivels your head, and only humans have it. So when filmmakers want to create a good alien, they often include this muscle to help viewers identify with the character.

Muscle Count

No one actually knows how many muscles there are in the human body. It all depends on how you count them. Massage specialists deal with about 200–300 skeletal muscles. But some anatomists might be able to identify another 400. Then there are millions of muscles that raise hairs, and billions of smooth muscles deep inside the body.

Bone Count

No one knows exactly how many bones you have right now! That's your body's secret. When you're born you have about 300, but as you grow, some of these bones fuse together. So by the time you're an adult you'll have just 206. Your bones also become denser and heavier until you're about 30 years old.

The Quiet Muscle

The tensor tympani is a tiny muscle in each of your ears. Its job is to pull on the tiny hammer bone in your ear and stop the bone from rattling when you're chewing. That way you aren't deafened by the sound of your own mouth. . . . It also stops your ears from getting damaged if you yell too loudly!

Sleep Power

We know how exercise can make your muscles grow. But *when* do the muscles actually grow after that tough workout? It seems that this happens when you fall into a deep sleep. Your muscles relax, allowing more blood to flow and the hormones that stimulate muscle growth to circulate.

Hot Muscle

Your muscles create a lot of your body heat. When muscles contract, they generate a lot of warmth. That's why you shiver when you are cold. Your body is trying to warm you up by rapidly contracting and relaxing muscles.

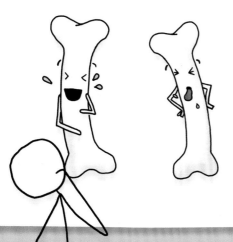

Funny Bone

People often talk of hitting their funny bone. It's actually not a bone at all. It's the ulnar nerve, which runs across your elbow on the inside. Accidentally bumping it sets off a strange, tingling sensation in your hand and arm.

INDEX

The Author

John Farndon is Royal Literary Fellow at City&Guilds in London, United Kingdom, and the author of a huge number of books for adults and children on science, technology, and nature, including such international best sellers as *Do Not Open* and *Do You Think You're Clever?*. He has been shortlisted six times for the Royal Society's Young People's Book Prize for a science book, with titles such as *How the Earth Works, What Happens When?*, and *Project Body* (2016).

The Illustrator

Venitia Dean is a freelance illustrator who grew up in Brighton, United Kingdom. She has loved drawing ever since she could hold a pencil! As a teenager she discovered a passion for figurative illustration, and when she turned nineteen she was given a digital drawing tablet for her birthday and started transferring her work to the computer. She hasn't looked back since! As well as illustration, Venitia loves reading graphic novels and walking her dog Peanut.

Picture Credits (abbreviations: t = top; b = bottom; c = center; l = left; r = right)
© www.shutterstock.com:

6 cl, 6 br, 7 tl, 7 cr, 7 bl, 8 bl, 9 tl, 9 cl, 9 bl, 17 cr, 21 bl, 23 br, 25 br, 26 bl, 28 bl, 29 bl.
6 br = Juan Aunion / Shutterstock.com
7 cr = meunierd / Shutterstock.com